IF THE WORLD BECOMES SO BRIGHT

2/7/2011

Douglas Lake, Mi.

for Ian —

see p. 8 —

and many thanks

for your work

In friendship,

Keith

IF THE WORLD BECOMES SO

Bright

POEMS BY KEITH TAYLOR

Keith Taylor

WAYNE STATE UNIVERSITY PRESS DETROIT

13 12 11 10 09   5 4 3 2 1

Library of Congress Cataloging-in-Publication Data

Taylor, Keith, 1952–
If the world becomes so bright : poems / by Keith Taylor.
p. cm. — (Made in Michigan writers series)
ISBN 978-0-8143-3391-4 (pbk. : alk. paper)
I. Title.
PS3570.A9418I34 2009
811'.54—dc22
2008029608

∞

This book is supported by the Michigan Council for Arts and Cultural Affairs

Designed and typeset by Maya Rhodes
Composed in Serlio LH and ITC Galliard

FOR MY DAUGHTER, FAITH

CONTENTS

CONDITIONS

If I jumped,
would I keep
my eyes open?
Look down
at the ground
coming up fast?
Or would I close
them, feel nothing
but the wind rush
past my ears,
blowing out loose
strands of hair?

If I'd gone bad—
     and I could have—
          and if I'd survived—
which is less certain—
     I would be fatter,
     hairier, dirtier,
     I'd be loud
     in public places.
     I'd be drunk
     by eight and act
     as if the world
          loved only me.

If I'd chosen
            to live like my friend
            Steve, I might
be eulogized
            by a farmer
                who would tell
the congregation
                how I drove
                out to the back field
behind the woods
            through grass
                    taller than my car
            one early fall morning
                        just to talk.

If I touched the sap
on the spruce out back
                        and left a print
or a bit of fingernail,
                some loose skin,
it might settle,
harden until the tree dies,
compress, become stone,
                get carried away
by new rivers
        or unimaginable explosions,
                and a different being
in a different world
                        might find it
millions of years from now
                        and polish it
for a piece of amber jewelry
        to decorate a child's bracelet
or the collar for some new pet.

If the offering we made
        to Pele, volcano goddess,
at the edge of Halemaumau
        on Kilauea—a small cairn
                and tobacco
from a broken cigarette—
                        doesn't work,
            will the piece of lava,
only one inch by two,
            from a recent flow—
        1984, I think—
            that sits now
    with other stones
in a basket on top
        of our television,
                    bring bad luck
or, worse yet,
                start glowing
        some quiet evening,
calling up its brothers
        and sisters from the Earth's
            hot core to join
in a midwestern fire?

If the world becomes so bright
        we can't see the stars,
will they become stories
                like mythical wars
                    or old gods?
        Or will we—
                all of us,
        the whole world—
           plan festivals—
say, six hours long,
        on the sixth new moon
of each bright year—
           when we turn off
        all our lights—
           every single bulb—
and dance quietly
        beneath temporary stars?

If Bill died—which
has not happened,
               at least, not yet—
I would be up-
               set, probably.
          I'd cry, would have
               trouble sleeping
for days, because
               I wouldn't have
               told him that of
my memories
                    one of the best
is staying up
too late in Greece,
          Olympia,
drinking ouzo—
               Bill, Christine, me—
and arguing
          all night about
                    apocalypse,
               explosions, the
end of the world.

Bill was certain
          it would happen
               soon, maybe on
the coming bright
               Peloponnesian
          morning, and I
                    wasn't so sure,
thought we might just

bumble through some
millennia
          still, when a tired
                    Englishman knocked
                    on our door, said
          Yes, I'm really
fascinated,
                    I'm enjoying
                              every word,
          every word.

If all this longing
for the end of the world,
the end of time, whatever,
is just a psychological quirk,
a head trick, and crumpled pages
from Shakespeare
never do blow across a dry
and lifeless planet,
what will happen?
Just the same old worries
about feeding the children,
washing dishes, mortgage
payments, and what
will we do if it rains?

If I forget everything
        when I'm old—
my wife, my daughter,
all the years
of work and travel—
          what will remain?
    One day, perhaps,
when I sat
      with my friend Dave—
and he is already
many years gone—
         below the walls
    at Carcassonne,
and we ate bread
    and cheese and sausage
that we sliced
      with a jackknife?
    My friend cut
his finger and we saw
    a dead rat
    in the grass.

If I sat in one place
            long enough,
                        looking out,
not in,
            I would see
                        many things—
            not everything—
                        but what came
                        would be
its own adventure—
            cement cracking
                        under the slow
pressure of weeds,
            children growing,
                        and the birds,
of course, coming
                        and going,
            flying over
                        or picking bugs
                        from my toes.

If I had the tongues
of angels,
        what would I say?
I do this, I do that?
                Here's my family?
Here's my house?
        Here's how I get my living?
Occasionally days come when
                there's nothing better
in this expanding universe
        than cherry cobbler?

If I see my daughter
       in the daylight world
as I saw her in my dream—
          grown, smiling
      and ruddy, standing
      in a corral, holding reins,
her hair windblown—
       will it be enough?

Our Mornings Won't Always Be Like This

THE 8:35 BUS

Our mornings won't always be like this.
Soon we'll find a little place to rent
out west of town, plant an acre garden
and stay home to fight invading aphids.
We'll build a cabin up north, where snow will keep
us in for weeks, feed evening grosbeaks
and learn the proper way to bank a fire
in our Peacock stove. We'll sail the North Atlantic
from Newfoundland to the Hebrides,
then tan slowly on beaches next to bodies
that will never know one day of work.
We'll measure the semicircle a falcon makes
migrating past our castle in Spain. We will
eat the golden peaches in Samarkand!

CASHIER'S DREAM; THE HUNT

At that moment, call it the float
if you like, but the precise moment
between your giving me the money
and my giving you the merchandise,
the thing you want or need,
for a small profit—a fair profit,
no one's getting rich here,
just enough to buy food or pay
for my children's clothes or the gas bill—
at that moment we have entered

the hunt, the clear air
of early morning—I have not
moved in an hour or more,
not even swallowed in fear
of frightening off the prey . . .
at that moment I launch
my spear or stone with prayers
that it bring down the brother—
my brother, my prey, you—

and before the bloodletting,
the skinning, I thank the gods
of the hunt, the spirit
of the beast, and I thank you
when you tuck whatever thing
I've sold you under your arm
and begin to leave, returning
to your careless ordinary day.

THE DAY AFTER AN ICE STORM

When it dawns crystalline, blue,
the air sparkling with prisms
reflected off oak and spruce,
off every twig, branch, or limb,
even off trees cascading
over fences, trees uprooted
by the splendor of ice—
the day lifts us, takes us out-
side ourselves, outside the news
of a nurse driving back home
last night, at the blackest hour
of the ice storm, when I was
watching electrical arcs
illuminating the yard.
I heard trees break apart
and was thrilled with fear. She stopped
to help at an accident—
it looked far worse than it was—
when a young man, twenty-three,
leaving work in his truck,
spun out on the ice killing
the nurse, who, in a brief moment
of faith, might have imagined
today dawning crystalline,
brittle, gloriously cold.

WEATHER REPORT

for Khaled Mattawa

You wouldn't believe the green.
It still startles me, so unexpectedly
there, outside the window
where I've learned to look
for winter. Grass, and the tips
of spruce branches, flower stems.
Crocuses have come and gone
already. Hyacinths and tulips
are in full bloom, daffodils
past their peak. Only last
week rain turned to snow
for a night and left a white
dusting on the pile of peat
beside the bed where Christine
is planting new perennials.
It's April. The weather's
flipping from early summer
to late winter and I can't
go two days without shouting
at people I don't know
about things I barely understand.
When the finches came
to our feeder this morning,
I saw they had finished
their molt, and seemed as bright
as your Mediterranean,
your desert sun. Even this

close to the Arctic we can't
go four months without
at least one blossom hidden
somewhere in our backyard.

They're Out There, Waiting

The man from the Humane Society said
don't trap skunks in June or July.
Babies, he said. Two to ten in a brood.
If you get the mother, the young stay
below and start stinking. Be patient.
Maybe she'll move if you make life hard—
so we stuck mothballs down the hole
and ammonia soaked rags, left
the backyard spotlight on all night,
and played rock 'n' roll on a portable
all day in the shed above her den.
Nothing worked. Finally we let her stay
under the floor where she built her home
just after the garden started to bloom.
We let her take the lily of the valley
and our Siberian iris. We gave her space
and let her be. But now her smell
rises at three a.m. We close
our windows and sweat till dawn.
Our shed stinks of musk, and we're afraid
to walk in the yard after dark. We stand
at the kitchen window and look out past
evening primrose and daylilies, wait
for rustling by the compost or ten sets
of stripes hurrying off to the empty lot
out back. But we don't see them. They know
their competition and have learned the rules.
Their paths crisscross our flower beds.

Stems and leaves shredded. The edge moves in,
and their smell rises everywhere like
nothing but the clear, sour odor of skunk.

OUTSIDE

for Stephen Leggett

OK. I'll entertain the possibility
that we have these long lives
purely to raise these coffee cups
at this moment in this one place
or that our purpose—if we need one—
may be to lift one half-drowned
yellow jacket from the birdbath,
set it on the lawn chair and watch
it buzz off to its nest in the back lot.
I'll admit the hope that we intersect
with everything—bee, oak, coffee cup—
in a glorious unnamed pattern.
But I can't turn one thing into any
other: the solitary bittern's call
rising from the marsh at dusk remains
the echoing call of one secretive bird
hidden behind a forest of dry rushes.
It is what it is and would be that
without my eyes or ears or my ability
to name it and find its place on any map.

AT THE WENDY'S EAST OF SALINE
for Anne Carson

Behind the back parking lot
close to the factory
that makes molded plastic parts—
bumpers, knobs and cup holders
for the big Ford pickup truck—
in a scrubby stand of oaks
next to a subdivision
of vinyl-sided houses,
a great horned owl peers
over the edge of her nest,
seemingly unperturbed,
as if she's been watching there
for two or three thousand years.

Detail from the Garden
of Delights

There's a way out. In the back
corner under mulberry bushes and a stand
of juniper, we hide with our familiar
spirits. We dance discreetly naked.

We are fed impossible raspberries
by a goldfinch who does all the work
and doesn't mind. We nestle into the down
on his back and drift into flying sleep.

If occasionally we are filled
with the common longing to look down
at new places, our hair turns red
and we ride a robin, windblown
only by the breeze from his wings.

We can see roseate spoonbills
on the backs of ewes, cows with paws.
No houses anywhere. No business.
No church. No school. An endless garden.

We kiss in the shade cast by a kingfisher,
who has come to watch, even though
our streams are buried and we offer
nothing but the spectacle of joy.

LIVY, ABRIDGED

Once I put the baby in her playpen
below our picture window and give her
the green alligator puppet to play
with, I can settle back for a minute
to read about Romulus organizing
shepherds into his city on the hills.
But she starts laughing loudly, and somewhere
between the rape of the Sabine women
and the Tarquinian machinations
to recapture the crown of Rome, I look
over to see her swaying, tentative
on her hands and knees, beginning her first
shuffle across the whole width of her pen.

Domestic Spirit

We have a ghost in our house,
a benevolent spirit
who protects us from minor
disasters—trees collapsing
our roof, water pipes bursting
in places where they could do
some real damage, basketballs
colliding with our windows.

We call him Mr. Sample
and understand he can't keep
off cancers or house fires caused
by rank carelessness, bad hearts,
the genuine tragedies
inevitable even
in a small house protected
by its own local spirit.

But we hear Mr. Sample
whispering in the walls
or along the creaking floor,
and when I turn the corner
by the new basement bookshelves
next to the washing machine,
I get the sense of his presence,
that he's watching and he cares.

MEMORIAL DAY

Past the trillium, the hostas
and mayapples, way the other
side of the oaks, my two neighbors
who "don't speak" sit in their yards
looking opposite directions.

They have their things to celebrate
so I don't call them over
to see the scarlet tanager
in the trees or the furious
hummingbird working the lilacs.

A MONK'S RULE
for Christine

But for you, my love,
I would take a monk's rule.
Rise long before dawn,
have a simple breakfast
of unbuttered toast and milk.
One cup of coffee, black.
I would go upstairs,
sit with paper and pen,
and plumb the deepest reaches
of my mind or soul or self.
Evenings I would read
nothing but books written
in the first millennium.

No Harm

If I've grown happy in a small house surrounded
by three oaks, two elms, one spruce, a redbud
I planted last spring, and fifty kinds of flowers,
if I get excited when warblers migrate
through my yard in early May or feel
the systole/diastole rhythm I take for granted
move uptempo when vagaries of wind and season
bring chimney swifts or an osprey overhead,
and if I want to call it all a kind of wisdom
even though I know it's regional and smug,
then let me be. I'm quiet and do no harm.

WHAT'S NEEDED NOW

Through a Crack in the World

I was a grand experiment. They had created
everything—trees, bodies, stars, water, time—just to
see how I would react. Nothing was as it appeared.
They had spent generations trying to convince
me that it was real. I was a good subject; usually I
believed in their creation. Their children—or their
equivalent for children, if they have youth, which
is doubtful—spent weeks—which, of course, they
don't have either—inventing the names for things.
Street, Atlantic, sister, thrush, Seattle. I lapped them
up. Originally they intended to take me out of the
definitions they had given me and bring me back to
reality. But they were too successful. Finally, they
realized that if I left the experiment I would crumble,
disappear. So they are stuck with me. They have to
watch even though they all lost interest long ago.
And I have to keep going, worrying about God and
the fall of the Roman Empire as if it all matters.
A couple of times—in an inexplicable hesitation
when my mother turned from a mirror or in an
inconsistency behind the eyes of a stranger on a city
street far from what I think of as home—I have seen
through a crack in the world to the laboratory wall,
white and gleaming, with windows. Behind them
move indistinct creatures without faces or names.

In the Other Life

I crouch, my back
against the outside
wall of the house
I made by braiding
branches together
until the rain
stayed out.
My wife and children
are sleeping inside.
I close my eyes
and feel the light
of our village fire
move in patterns
through the dark.
I still carry
the weight of today's
work, still feel
the warmth of water
around my calves,
the suck of mud
on my feet.
Everyone I know
is tired and here,
eyes closed,
listening through the hiss
of flames to a story
about a white beast
sleeping in shade below

a rock in a valley
far from here,
surrounded by mountains
none of us, not
even the storyteller,
will ever see.

LITTER ON THE NARRATIVE ARC

When I set off to kill a man
or before our marriage broke
into the shards that would cut us
for a dozen years or more,
I watched an awkward bird pick
apart bark from a dying birch,
then drove past a woman leaning
on her cane. Her only child left
town decades ago and moved west
to a temperate place where homes
have flower boxes stuffed with red
geraniums. He never writes.

WHAT'S NEEDED NOW

May 31, 1998

            I am willing
to let the impressions come
with their various degrees
of intensity, sometimes
vague, sometimes as sharp and as
multilayered as Basho's
haiku—
            the dog, alert, her
ears twitching at the Sunday
traffic on the street; the tops
of the three black walnut trees
in the neighbor's yard swaying
in the gusts of wind hanging
around after a thunder-
storm blew through late last evening;
the dull ache in my head brought
on by late onset allergies
that's keeping me from any
good reading; the ticktocking
of the grandfather clock out
in the kitchen.

            Next week's my
forty-sixth birthday and that will be
exactly eleven months
since I quit smoking. I've tried

to blame this problem I've been
worried about—the problem
of focus—on a lack of
cigarettes. Usually
I blame all the extra weight
I'm carrying on the same
thing, so I should be careful
about where I look in my
slightly desperate search for
reasons.
                    (Right now I'm watching
a hockey game—Detroit and
Dallas, of all places—so
it's hard to concentrate on
my inability to
find a focus.)
                    (Period's
over. Detroit's still winning.)

Out on the back deck now,
my mind a television
glaze (but Detroit won), watching
the dog, halfheartedly, to
make sure she doesn't shit next door.
The ground is littered with white
peony petals, battered
off their flowers by a quick
rainstorm that hit us hard this
afternoon while Christine and I
had taken a little break

to make some daylight love up-
stairs. We were just coming when
the rain started—one of those
Shakespearian moments when
the outside world, parched and hot,
reflects the emotional
condition of the people
in the play. The heat's gone now,
broken. The air's fresh and light.
A breeze rustles the oak leaves.

       So how does one, do I,
does anyone maintain his
or her focus, not to write
novels or to paint pictures,
necessarily, but just
to think clearly about one
particular thing, even
a simple thing, extended
thinking, or perhaps some long
watching of something, any
thing, when dinner dishes must
be washed and the dog walked?
I've been closer in my past
and I remember how fresh
I felt—like walking into
a field after the first frost
or walking through a city
at dawn, one where I couldn't speak
the language and didn't need to.

That all sounded a lot
like closure, as if I were
beating the drum at the end
of some artistic thing, song
or poem, and there isn't an end
to this, unless of course I
achieve an epiphany
and learn, finally, the way
to direct my mind and my
imagination toward
a particular image
whenever that image calls
out for notice, when even
the smallest thing—peony
petal, jack-in-the-pulpit,
or bloodroot; robin, house finch,
or black-throated blue warbler—
sings to me with the power
of Gabriel's trumpet . . .

June 1, 1998

. . . calling for the end of time
or the beginning of some
new unimaginable
moment. But today is just
Monday, normally a day
off for me, a time to sit
around home, read, or download

my e-mail, but the other
managers at Shaman Drum
have all gone to Chicago
for BookExpo so I came
into town to run the weekly
and monthly reports and count
the money into the cash
drawers. Now I'm grabbing some
time, a few minutes, to sit
in a coffee shop and count
syllables and think about
the deadness in my head and
the focus I can't seem to
find to bring me out of my
narcissism and help me
reconnect with the good things
of this world.
                    And this focus
I'm belaboring here isn't
just one of art, though trying
to learn the art may have taught
me the importance of this
attention to small worldly
things, the precious objects that
surround us, and once knowing
that attention I miss it
terribly when I can't force
myself to give it. I can
worry that I won't feel it
again in this life. Just this
morning I felt the whisper

of pain in my chest. I have
already outlived my friends—
David Bray dead for almost
thirteen years now, Mike Simpson
for almost ten—and they were
both in much better shape than
me, chubby ex-smoking book-
seller that I am. So I
could drop at any moment,
even on a bright and clear
morning in early summer
when I had to count money
and prepare to read stories
before an audience of
high school juniors out at
Huron High. I've expected
it—the sudden blockage, stopped
breath—for years now. I'm amazed
it hasn't happened yet.

                    Now
the day is almost over.
I did the high school gig, mowed
the lawn, swept the drive and watched
Faith and her friend. The day has
been a good one with lots of
different tasks extending
the hours.
            I'm in the back-
yard, listening to the birds, watching

the sun play through the leaves. If
I could I would catalog
the myriad shades of green—
the green of spruce under oak,
sunlight through silver maple.
The Buddha might not approve,
but I am clinging to this
as if my life depended
on it. Which it does. It does.

All this longing to end!
It seems as if every
page has its ending. I must
fight the thing to keep going.
It wants to stop despite my
plan—the form I see for it:
which is this: last Saturday
I did a quick talk at a
writer's conference where all
of us were given fancy
tote bags in which were notebooks
and pens—this notebook, this pen.
Though just an ordinary
college spiral notebook, it
has a surprising firmness
to it, a sturdiness that
attracted me right away.
On the outside it says there
are eighty sheets inside it,
which in my math means there are

160 sides
in it, and I've been having
this problem of focus—if
you remember (who is "you"
and where did he or she come
from? Am I suddenly and
rashly imagining that
someone will actually
read this? Will that imagined
reader change things or was he
or she there all along and
I just couldn't face the thought?)
—so for twenty-four hours I
kicked around the idea
of filling all these nine-and-
one-half by six-and-one-half
pages, all eighty sheets, that's
160 sides,
with my search for this focus.
But I'm just finishing up
page ten now—one-sixteenth of
the project—and the thing has
tried to end itself at least
three times already, as if
it were some kind of song
or poem, some work of art that
resolved everything nicely.
That is not what I need now.

APOLOGIA

We shrink the palette, some of us anyway,
until things get simple, like those few paintings
by Monet where he dispensed with sunsets
and cathedrals and seemed content doing snow.

Somber, write the curators about mauve, blue,
flat green, and white, as if, dull souls, they've never
breathed cold air, felt it sharp and dry,
lively as a knife deep in their humid lungs.

Ten steps back and canvas becomes photograph;
twenty, and it disappears—but somewhere out there
waits the exultation of the cracking ice,
the shiver and the fear just before a thaw.

FAITH AT THE EDGE OF WINTER

a renga

1.
Summer's last full moon—
cicada hum at midnight
drowns next-door music.

2.
Not them—they're asleep, thank God.
It's those folks across the street.

3.
Black walnuts drop—
small green explosions—
on car tops.

4.
Hailstones flash in sun,
then melt.

5.
Spruce boughs, bent,
lift back
toward sky.

6.
Snow piles
grow in the shade.

7.
The bald man whistles
shoveling out
his drive.

8.
His son's gone off to college.
His wife winters somewhere south.

9.
She sleeps beneath banana trees—
an ocean laps
her chair.

10.
Water over rocks—
white fire.

11.
In camp above the river—
fire burns down,
first frost settles in.

12.
Aurora—green, white—
rising from every horizon.

13.
Morning sun in May
hits trillium—white petals
glow in our dark corner.

14.
Migrating white-throated sparrows
call, delicately.

15.
Rain at Height of Land—
bird song, unrecognized,
unseen in thimbleberry thickets.

16.
Cold feet on New Year's—
new bird in the pines!

17.
Hepatica, spring beauty,
gallant
through oak leaf mulch.

18.
Wind rustles the last brown leaves.
One twists down and slaps our grass.

19.
First cry
in back bedroom.
Our winterborn child.

20.
We've hope, snow, windblown leaves,
some warmth, a distant spring.

21.
The jet stream
falls:
December freeze.

22.
Who thinks
about new flowers?

23.
Retired preacher
limping through the park
jumps over sidewalk cracks.

24.
Mother flips in her grave.
Joy or pain?

25.
Faith at the edge of winter,
in old migrations:
yellow warblers coming back!

26.
Three note song—sweet, sweet, sweet—
from early sumac, autumn olive.

27.
Imported for a colonial hedge:
alien connections
in a second growth forest.

28.
Every starling on this continent—
all the birds in Shakespeare!

29.
Two hundred lift—
breathing silhouette
against a gray sky.

30.
After years of yellow winters,
snowfall, finally, up past my knees.

31.
Cat in the window
looks out
between African violets.

32.
Pink, purple—wild in some place
we won't see anytime soon.

33.
Full moon there—
faint shard of light
through the high canopy.

34.
Dream of cold
in a country constantly warm!

35.
What's the first shoot
of crocus
through dirty snow?

36.
A father carries his daughter
into her first spring.

This Fall's Murder
after Snyder

For a couple of weeks in the fall, crows gather in
the black oaks that grow in and around our backyard.
They come in after their days picking apart roadkill or
hamburger buns by the dumpster behind the Burger
King on Stadium. They arrive in late afternoon and
stay in the tops of the trees, skittish, their shit hitting
the downed leaves like an irregular rainstorm. By
nightfall, they fly off to join the larger gatherings, the
kind that get written up in the local paper. 10,000
Crows in the St. Thomas Cemetery! 15,000 Crows
by Angell Hall Create Hazard on Sidewalk!

My daughter thinks I'm insane when I go out the
back door clapping and yelling—*HUNH, HUNH,
HUNH*—as loud as I can, and the crows rise in a
black swirl, squawking and circling. She thinks the
neighbors might call the cops about the crazy guy
running through the neighborhood clapping at
crows.

I don't do it to get rid of them. They come back
anyway, and leave in their own good time. I don't
think I do it to torture crows. I do it just because I
like to see the group of them rise into the evening
sky, noisy black against a gray sky.

The crows are forming this fall's murder
in our black oaks out back. Their droppings
are smeared on the sidewalk and our car.

When I clap and yell, they rise, squawk,
and fly off complaining. They circle
back soon enough, settle in again,
muttering incomprehensible
syllables like demented old men.

After I'd written those few lines, I sent them
off to an old acquaintance, a man who had lived
and worked here for many years and who hated the
place the whole time. As soon as he could, he retired
and moved back to New England, where he is quite
happy now, remembering his entire professional life
as an exile in an ugly place among difficult people.
I thought my lines had some affection for this place
and its crows, but after reading them my friend back
East wrote, "Yes, that's how I remember the crows in
that place. Here our crows are sleek and beautiful."

DIRECTIONS TO NORTH
FISHTAIL BAY

No Beginning

Just woke up
one almost bright day
on this freeway
with exit signs
to towns
I've never heard of

The Road from Galahad

The boy who became the preacher who became
my father first saw God in a snowstorm
while he walked, hunched against the weather,
north on the road from Galahad, Alberta.

God-smacked, like Paul, while walking home
for evening chores, he fell to his knees right there
on frozen gravel next to a frozen slough
on a Sunday night. March, 1936.

Soon enough the slough would fill with willets,
marbled godwits, and canvasback ducks dodging
coyotes and breeding furiously before they flew
their long routes back to Caribbean beaches,

but this night whatever the boy saw in the snow
drifting against fence posts, snow so thick
it lightened the sky, whatever he saw was enough
to sustain him through that century of doubt.

All the Time You Want

Take the chain from the gate. Walk in.
No one really cares. Most of the stones
have faded, are cracked or broken.

Designed as a churchyard
like the ones left behind
in the Old Country, the yard

outlasted its church. All the kids
who could moved to town years ago.
Someone mows, but not often.

Here you are free to invent
whatever tales you need.
Please, take all the time you want.

See that obelisk, barely a yard tall
tilting over in the back corner,
about to fall—it marks

another common story: early death,
illness and a miserable marriage.
If you think you have some time,

you can pick weeds from the plot
or try to right that stone.
There's little else to do here.

FOR MARILYN AND THE ROOTCELLAR

She was a year older
and knew things
so I had followed her

here, deep into the center
of the only hill
in our prairie lives.

I held the light, slightly shaking,
while she brushed the shavings aside
and unearthed two potatoes

buried below roots
for warmth, still slowly growing
in memory of summer.

She cut the nubs away,
peeled back the skin
to potato whiteness,

and here, in the one place
we were told never to visit,
we shared the raw food
we were told never to touch.

CLASS JUMPING AT
CHATEAU LAKE LOUISE

Royalty stops here. Rich American
Buddhists pay thousands for seven-day retreats
to learn the advanced method for counting breath.
This is not a place my family slept.
We would walk through the tulips,
take pictures of the *Please Stay Off the Grass* signs
(in French and English), of the lake, its turquoise
never quite captured in our slides,
of the mountains and glaciers.
We bought souvenir spoons in the shops
before returning to the cheap cabins in the valley.
The liveried bellhops looked right over us,
but that was OK: we didn't know enough
to care, knew we didn't belong anyway
in those places where the wealthy vacationed.
Now, just off season and carrying Gold Cards,
I insist we spend a night, my own revenge,
and all the help is generous, even kind.

Landscape, 1963: The Rocks

Maybe I was mooning over a girl . . .
I don't really remember . . . but I rode
out east of town, to the Rosebud River.
It was just a stream, barely a yard wide.
I climbed through a fence, crossed a beaver dam,
and trudged up through poplars to a sandstone
outcropping: boulders and ragged pillars
weathered into hollows, cirques, hidden caves.
I leaned back against sandstone and looked out
across the valley into the evening.
A herd of mule deer—six, seven, then twelve—
hopped up the hill, springing like cartoon deer
(did I know they could do this?) until they
reached the fence at the top, just silhouettes
now against the evening sky, gracefully
hopping outlines easily vanishing
between the last barbed-wire fence and the sun.

The Hunting Camp: Before Dishes

I was alone in the cook tent waiting
for the water to boil. Old John had left
the pistol by his placemat. There'd been bear.
With time to kill before I could do
the breakfast dishes and because nothing quite
focuses attention like a pistol
on a table, because I was seventeen
and in love with anguish, I put it
in my mouth. I made sure the safety
was on and held it with both hands,
my thumbs firmly outside the trigger guard.
I stared cross-eyed down the barrel.

WATCHING

an immature white ibis
over the marsh at Hatteras
stretch awkwardly into
the wind at Hatteras
and come down to a pool
to jab his down-curved bill
into water on the coldest
day of the coldest March
in the memory of ibis
or any other creature
at Hatteras and pull up
one silver fish and throw
it back down his gullet
while the ocean wind
around Hatteras stings
ibis and blurs the eyes
of whatever else might
be there in March
at Hatteras watching
an immature white ibis

THE FIT IN WEST CLARE
for Thomas Lynch

I mispronounce the place names
here, and when your neighbors greet
us, sometimes I think it could
be easier if they would
simply speak Greek.

When I got up in the night
to piss, I didn't put on
my glasses in the faint hope
that blurry vision might help
me see a ghost.

Instead I stubbed my big toe
on the raised flagstone in front
of the new bedroom. I know
you know these hauntings never
arrive when planned.

I did do one job and kept
a running tally of birds
seen by the cottage, the road,
the Shannon estuary
on one side, on the other
the Atlantic.

Thirty-six species so far.
The ones we don't have back home

get me excited, of course:
pied wagtail or meadow pipit,
fulmar, stone chat.

But there's a certain pleasure
in the familiar, the wren
(*Troglodytes troglodytes*)
that flew into the entryway,
that porch designed to hold
rubber boots soiled by work
in the cow fields.

Back home in Michigan we call it
winter wren because—though we may
have fewer ghosts—we have more
species of wren. My daughter
caught it in her hands and let
it go in the green bushes
by the turf shed.

She took great pleasure naming
the small bird that collided
with the north window: blue tit.
Like our chickadee, I said.
And she said, *Just try to get
that one in a poem,* and laughed
all through dinner.

The locals assume we have
ancestral connections here
and my Polish Catholic
wife claims I do . . .

But I'm a bit more worried
about centuries of hate
and feel the need to point out—
Scots-Irish—then think they think:
a Protestant!

So we fit imperfectly
here in your wet parishes,
although when I went to wash
the jeans I have worn all week
I realized that they were yours,
just one size too large—

I thought that maybe I lost
an inch on my long working
vacation in Greece and France,
but no such luck.

When we went on the dolphin
watch out of Carrigaholt,
the woman selling tickets
asked—when she found out we were
staying up at the Lynch place
in Moveen—if I might not
be a brother or a cousin.
She thought, just maybe, I looked
like family.

BIRTHDAY ON MT. WASHINGTON

At fifty-one I'm satisfied to be
the slowest hiker on the slope,
satisfied to stop somewhere below
the summit's restaurant and parking lot
where others are pleased to see
the view from the highest place
on this part of their planet, mountains
falling off around them, blue and green,
in all directions. I'm satisfied
to keep my hike pristine,
if artificially so, satisfied
to sit at the bottom of a sea
of rock covering the quarter mile
to the top, to sit above the last
alpine meadow, beginning to bloom
just this month—purple lapland rosebay
as backdrop to diapensia:
small, white, threatened by the noisy world.
And I feel something
more than satisfaction—not
"euphoria," but that direction—
when a ruby-throated hummingbird
zooms up the rocks, circles
my head looking for blossoms, darts down
over cliffs and krummholz balsam fir,
then dives for the flowered slopes below.

June 4, 2003

The Failure of Imagination

While climbing Chocorua, I reached
the point where I thought I would make it—
despite rain and clouds, profoundly soaked
in sweat—just past the worst slippery rocks.
The mountain in imagination:
there, contained, completed by my climb.

The mist and clouds below me opened
for a moment on the hills and woods,
the little white houses and their fields
disappearing into all the miles
between us; I grew dizzy then:
middle-aged, overweight, out of place.

Another Coole
for Jerry Dennis

Rafts of goldeneyes float on the east arm
of Grand Traverse Bay, just past the ice cones
and between the small ice flows pushed north
toward the open lake. Too many to count!
I sit in a house of cut stone, hand-hewn
timber, and polished columns of white oak,
receiving the generosity
of the well heeled, like those generations
of poets occasionally pampered
in the castles of Europe, the palaces
of India—a couple of days, a month,
sometimes a year, before they were sent out,
once again, to wander from here to there,
from love to new love, in the pelting rain
and the wind, to lose themselves in the snow.

An Afternoon at Lake Michigan

We, too, are Sunday people, even though we rent
our rooms each night and sleep miles from the lake.
Avoiding villages with art galleries, we hike
in to nearly empty beaches where sailboats
are far enough out to look scenic. Like
everyone else we turn slowly raw beneath the sun
and listen to the erotic wash of waves lessen
in this afternoon calm. We, too, wait
for the electric whine inside to dull,
for the dog monkeying around the breakers to come
and shake wet sand on our blankets and books.

A WALK

1.

. . . from that place in a hall in an old farmhouse,
at the foot of a narrow stairway that rose
up to darkness at the top—no one believes
I can remember my first steps; *you heard it
from your family,* they say, but I remember
I was alone and no one saw the things I saw;
I know a man who remembers his own birth,
I say, who remembers pain when he was pushed
into his life—and I pulled myself upright
by that stairway, turned and walked, uncertainly
of course, back to the living room and the light.

2.

. . . on New Year's Eve after I snuck out of church—
the Watch Night Service where my family watched
minutes crawl, sang hymns, and prayed until midnight—
and outside in air so cold it hurt to breathe,
air that rose up dense and smoky around me
when I walked fast, faster over the snow
crunching back at me, until I was running,
exhilarated, until the twelve bells chimed
and the drunk and godless yelled through their windows
to the boy running by—*Happy New Year, kid!*—
and all I wanted was to join the party.

3.

. . . alone from the East Station to the river,
then west through courtyards and the palace gardens—

and somewhere here among the fountains the sun
finally broke through the trees, over the shops
and hotels onto the first old man reading
his morning paper on a bench wet with dew—
to the Fields of Heaven and all the way up
to the Place of the Star—and I understood,
or thought I did for a minute, maybe two,
the notion that the sun might need one of us
each morning (and this morning it might be me)
to bring it back over the crest with the power
of our joy—and I returned to the river
to stand in line before the sparkling tower.

4.
. . . in the Manistee National Forest
on snowshoes, probably four feet on the ground
already and more snow falling, and I lost
direction out in the scrub oak and jack pine,
then wandered for hours hearing only raven
croaks and the deceptively close nuthatch calls,
nasal and metallic, until I stumbled
upon a snowed-under, fire-access, two-track road
I vaguely remembered and found my way back
to my friends, their cabin, their woodstove and fire.

UPPER PENINSULA FIRES

A hundred miles north the forest is burning.
Smoke drifts down this far at night and just at dawn
I smell something like wet charcoal in my cabin.
Sunsets glow deeper red and spectacular
the longer the fire burns, the more the peat,
cracked and brittle, and those cedars in their dry swamps
smolder into the autumn of a parched year.

DIRECTIONS TO NORTH FISHTAIL BAY

If you paddle down past
the point where the eagles
hang out, you're almost there.
It's best like this—a hint
of fog flittering across
the lake before a breeze.
No sun, sky gray, but calm,
not a ripple or a wave.
Just round the next point, where
the sand drops away fast
under luminous deep green
water . . . And you made it!
Go now. It looks like rain.

You'll hear a hermit thrush
calling, hidden in the pines
or in a cedar swamp
where, when you look hard
into the dark, you will see
a profusion of iris,
almost purple and fresh
on this day, the very day you've
come alone to North Fishtail Bay.
There's thunder in the west.
Go now. It looks like rain.

DREAM OF THE BLACK WOLF: NOTES FROM ISLE ROYALE

Once Chuang Chou dreamt he was a butterfly, a butterfly flitting and fluttering around, happy with himself and doing as he pleased. He didn't know he was Chuang Chou. Suddenly he woke up and there he was, solid and unmistakable Chuang Chou. But he didn't know if he was Chuang Chou who dreamt he was a butterfly, or a butterfly dreaming he was Chuang Chou. Between Chuang Chou and a butterfly there must be some distinction!

—CHUANG TZU
Translated by Burton Watson

Between Home and Isle Royale

The world is such that I can't
say where, exactly, the place
is or some overzealous
botanist might travel there
to collect the last flower,
and I can't even name it—
although the name's a good one,
worth remembering—because
I promised the friend who took
me there I wouldn't tell it,
but I'll say it's by a lake,
a big lake—and our country
has many lakes—somewhere
between home and Isle Royale,
and it has a small flower,
yellow, easily overlooked,
growing from green clumps of leaves
at the edge or even
in the middle of cold streams,
never warmer than forty-
five degrees, spring-fed streams
that seldom freeze in winter,
and small rooted strands break off
from time to time, float downstream
and start another clump but
not often because this plant
grows in only four places
on Earth and we need special
knowledge or friends to find it.

I'm here. Looking out the front window of the cabin they've provided for me. Tobin Harbor. Isle Royale. Lake Superior. The only sound other than birdcall and the occasional outboard is the high ringing of my own blood in my ears. A family of mergansers has been playing in the calm water of the passage between this window and the little island fifty or sixty yards offshore. A loon floats through but doesn't sing. A black duck paddles past, its bill almost phosphorescent, greenish yellow. Two spotted sandpipers fly by. Chipping sparrows are nesting in the spruce not fifteen feet from the front door of this place. A late wild iris has bloomed in the four hours since I arrived. Two hours ago it was still wrapped around itself.

The Guest Cabin
for EK

Blue burns in a blue world.
Wild iris—the blue flag—
uncurled in a basalt crack
below spruce and beard moss.
A greeting, if we want it,
from the woman, long dead,
who built her place where
the wail and tremolo
of loon song collect
like the vespers chants
of monks moving to prayer.
At evening the sun prisms
through their windows dappling
the altar red and blue.

CANOEING AGAINST THE WIND

I don't have to do this

two strokes to move a yard

then a breath   a breeze   pushed
back and sideways against rocks

and my hat blows away

two strokes to move a yard

if this canoe were keeled
it wouldn't catch the wind
blowing from Superior
up the inlet   pushing

two strokes to move a yard

I'm here because I want
to be   I want to be

out in the wind

I canoed down Tobin Harbor, passed through Merritt Lane, and went out as far as I dared into the big lake. I didn't go very far, maybe a couple of hundred yards. Superior was quiet, but that water had a different quality than the water in the inlet or on the rivers I've canoed. There was power underneath toying with the canoe as it floated over the swales. I turned back to the island and beached the canoe on the rocks below Blake Point.

I climbed out to the point, sat and rested, looking toward Passage Island, three miles off. A few days ago a fisherman told me that he had seen a white pelican out there.

So I imagine sitting here, warm in the sun and tired after paddling, and seeing a white pelican flying straight in, a white giant with pure black wing tips. But it won't happen today. It won't happen at any moment I expect it.

Upstream on the Seiche

Carried upstream on the seiche—
water pushed back toward the source—
until the flow turns and my canoe
stalls on mud banks. Alder thickets,
mosquitoes and deer flies. Robins laugh
from the shade. I can do nothing
but slog back, pulling my boat
through slime, slapping at bugs.

Then, high in the mud . . . tracks.

I climb up, kneel before them
and sketch one in my notebook
to compare with a guide at home:
two and three-quarters wide;
three and three-quarters long;
angular toes, the center two
noticeably larger than the two outside.
The track of a small wolf,
its outline clear, the edges sharp,

until the seiche returns and fills
the creek, releasing my canoe.
Water rises to wolf print,
dissolving it, dirt stirred up
then back toward the big lake,
a gentle pull but strong enough
to carry me out past mud banks,

the sedge and rushes, jewelweed
glowing orange, oxeye daisies,
out past the thickets, shaded
at midday, creatures hiding inside.

Dream of the Black Wolf

A quick glimpse

            in my eye's
            corner—

black wolf
     running
            always running

    ears back
    fur
            shaggy
            hackles up
            a touch
                       of white
                       or silver

on its belly

beside the lake
over rock
and lost
         between spruce
         and cedar

         before
I turn

Two Days

The last walk to Lookout Louise, climbing
through ridges forced up by ice, then the view
across to Ontario, Thunder Bay
hazy from north shore fires and a small burn
here, over on Minong Ridge, sizzling
dried lichen, grasses, a few dead spruce.
And back down toward water . . . a bull moose,
not twenty yards from the trail. I shrink
beside him, in the shade and weight of rock.

Next morning the island shrinks, lost like a dream
in mist, as our ship pulls back toward Houghton
and the other dream, our dailiness,
a reality, I suppose, as hard
as island rock, separated
only by one night, a fitful sleep.

The last morning, just before dawn, while I was packing the canoe, a cow moose waded out into the little bay behind the cabin. She walked out as far as she could, then took off swimming. The sun broke over the trees on the opposite side of Tobin Harbor, and the moose was lost in the glare of sun on water.

I would like to be cold and clearheaded about these events, but it is hard not to take them as signs.

ACKNOWLEDGMENTS

Many of these poems first appeared—often in different forms or under different titles—in *Bear River Review, Bird Watcher's Digest, Bonfire Review, Driftwood, Generator, Hartland Poetry Quarterly, I Stay Home, Iowa Review, Michigan Quarterly Review, Notre Dame Review, Parting Gifts, Passages North, Phoebe, Pivot, Poetry in Performance (CCNY), Southern Review, Witness,* and *Wooster Review.*

"Landscape, 1963: The Rocks" first appeared in *In Drought Time; Scenes from Rural and Small Town Life* (Mayapple Press, 2005).

"At the Wendy's East of Saline" and "Upper Peninsula Fires" first appeared in *Writers Reading at Sweetwaters* (Words 'n' Woman Press, 2007).

"All the Time You Need" was commissioned by Evan

Chambers for inclusion in *The Old Burying Ground,* a song cycle for folk singer, soprano, and tenor, 2007.

"Faith at the Edge of Winter" first appeared in its entirety in an online holiday post of Dan Wickett's Emerging Writers Network, December 2008.

"Dream of the Black Wolf: Notes from Isle Royale" first appeared as a slightly longer version in a chapbook of the same title (Ridgeway Press, 1993). The author particularly acknowledges the work of M. L. Liebler at that press. Several sections of it were reprinted in *The Island Within Us: Isle Royale Artists in Residence, 1991–1998* (Isle Royale Natural History Association, 2000).

Many of these poems were first drafted as part of a 500-poem postcard sequence for the Alternative Press. The author continues to acknowledge the support and encouragement of Ken and Ann Mikolowski.

"For Marilyn and the Rootcellar" appeared in the chapbook *Learning to Dance* (Falling Water Books, 1985).

"Weather Report" appeared in the chapbook *Weather Report* (Ridgeway Press, 1988).

"The 8:35 Bus," "Cashier's Dream; The Hunt," "In the Other Life," "Outside," "Livy, Abridged,"

"They're Out There, Waiting," "No Harm," "Detail from the Garden of Delights," and two sections from "Conditions" appeared in the chapbook *Detail from the Garden of Delights* (Limited Mailing Press, 1993).

"Watching," "An Afternoon at Lake Michigan," and a small section of "Faith at the Edge of Winter" (under the title "White Fire") appeared in the chapbook *Everything I Need* (March Street Press, 1996).

Some of this work was completed with the help of fellowships from the National Endowment for the Arts and the Michigan Council for the Arts and Cultural Affairs. Some was completed with residencies at Isle Royale National Park and with the Writer's Voice at the Detroit YMCA.

The author admits that he would be lost in a dark wood without the help of Tom Fricke, Thomas Lynch, Raymond McDaniel, Annie Martin, John Repp, and Marc Sheehan. He also acknowledges, with deep gratitude, the assistance of Steven Gillis.